CW00502205

# trimming the wick

## laboni islam

ignitionpress

First published in 2023
by **ignition**press
Oxford Brookes Poetry Centre
Oxford Brookes University
OX3 OBP

Cover design: Flora Hands, Carline Creative


A CIP record for this book is available
from the British Library


ISBN 978-1-7399058-9-7

# Contents

*for my family,*
*in memory of my grandparents*
*and my father*

# Salt

*for my maternal grandmother, Nurun Nahar, who started the story*

[BANGLADESH]

These days, the sea adds salt to everything.
But I remember when my father gathered us daughters.
He was an old king, whose body curved into a question:

> *How do you love me?*

The way he asked us, so Shakespearean.

> *Like sugar.*
> *Like sugar,*

said my sisters, their voices swaying like the sweet cane.
This pleased the old king, who turned to me.

> *Like salt,*

said I, seawater evaporating from my tongue, my voice crystalline.
I knew my father's moods by the way they made landfall:

> *Like salt?*
> *Like SALT!*

I scrambled inside myself to survive the cyclone.
My silence, a suitable shelter.

With the cooks I spoke, negotiating the evening meal.
They took salt out of the *dal*, the *bhat*, the *bhaji*, the *aloo*, the *maach*,
   the *korma*, the *chutney*.
My father learned salt's worth by its absence.

But these days, the sea adds salt to everything —

1

mangroves standing sentry at the coastline know the sea
is moving inland, salting the fields so rice stops growing,
salting the wells, so water is undrinkable.

I would take salt out of the wells, the fields.

And if the old king asked again: *How do you love me?*
I would say my love is a complicated country, barely above sea level.

## Low-Lying Country

         watch
sea level rise like fever spilling
over
        mudlines.  everything
stilts itself.


Jamuna.  Meghna.  Padma.
to live alluvially near three rivers rising
     or


in slums with more than miles can hold
is to choose


between catastrophes.


          Child
    remember water was your first teacher—

knot
      your resilience
        around your waist.


  dis-
mantle your tilting house     move
         farther and farther from the shoreline
      an open parenthesis
    where cyclones whirling through names will eventually
      make landfall on yours
        (your field left open, flooded

# An Animal in a Two-Piece Shell

*a found poem*

Your shell may grow rapidly,
one half
a mirror image of the other.

Bury your hinge
and mantle in seabed, or
move between tide marks.

Live out your brief life
unseen, undisturbed, unsuspected
by the casual observer.

When you die,
your shape and ornament
will wash ashore.

And the living
will consider the history
of the once-living organism,

the nomenclature
of your body.

## Girl Made of Shells

Like flood tide my mother returns from the Bay of Bengal
and brings me a girl made of shells.
She is a figure of flutes and whorls who carries the sound of the sea.


Every shell built by a soft animal
that wore its toughness on the outside:
her feet coquinas,
her body, moon shell and olive,
her arms small augers,
and her face is a cowrie that camouflaged
to survive life in the reef.


I hold the girl made of shells in my hand like an inheritance.
Two brows form a black gull flying
over her eyes' dark coasts.
Only a trace of a mouth.


It is easier to write about a girl made of shells
than to write about being a girl.


As a cowrie, her face has a history as currency,
light and portable and marriageable.
Or made into jewellery
to adorn.

My grandmother taught my mother

and my mother taught my sister and me

a game we are playing

together across time. I toss


four cowries into a ring:

If they all land with their mouths closed,

I earn one point apiece.

Mouths open, double for each one

I grab before others do.

Three alike, a missed turn.

Two alike, I flick shells

with open mouths against closed—


See how the cowries glance

off each other.


See how we cast our faces

into the game.

## Lunar Eclipse

I audition for the part of the Moon: airless, become
a surface unliveable, over four billion years young
with a white-hot ball bearing of a heart. My situation
is concentric. Life's a lit elliptical. I spin-spin and
orbit Earth, which spin-spins and orbits the Sun's
swift furnace. Effort returns me to my starting place.
*La la la la la la.* I have mixed feelings about gravity:
On one hand, it keeps me here. On the other hand,
it keeps me here. Everyone's familiar with my phases
but forgetful of my seas. Oh, my maria! Named
*cleverness* named *serenity* named *crises* named *fertility.*
Earth casts a shadow, which I enter involuntarily.
Penumbra. Umbra. Why is everyone's interest in me
greatest when I am disappearing?

# On the First Day of Ramadan

She woke before dawn
to indigo hours, wide and silent as a yawn. It was spring, that time
    of year
when days were long and lengthening like her hair, gathered
and pinned neatly as an intention: She would fast,
which was both a choice and a promise, broken easily
as eggs over a skillet. The first hours, her hunger
hardly moved, tucked in as the sun rose
lifting dark sheets from the suburb.
By the sixth hour, hunger had rooted in the moist soil of her belly,
an adolescent hunger, more than seedling but less than tree. By the
    tenth hour,
her hunger had a hundred rings, was tall and windward leaning
like the spruce beyond her balcony.
Long had she loved that spruce and known its silhouette.
In the fourteenth hour, four fellers and a bright strategy
of vests assembled in the yard. They were staring at the spruce,
a stance she recognized, because by then
she was downhill from her hunger looking up at it.
They roped the spruce's crown
of needle and cone and the crown bowed, slightly. Soon came the whir
of blade and chain, sawing back through years
to early rings. When the spruce fell, the ribs of the day
gave way to its dark and scaly bark, all the sun at work inside its cells,
whorls of needles fastened to their twigs. As she watched,
she felt her hunger topple too,
felled by the cool metal of time's sharp teeth.
Armful by armful, they carried its limbs
to the helix and drum of quick machinery. They split
the trunk into logs. She felt her hunger reduced and stacked to the side.
It took four fellers, two trucks, one chainsaw, one chipper, one
    grinder, and one long
coil of rope to make that tree disappear.
A windstorm weeks earlier. Some said the spruce was dangerous
but there was a rumour, you see, that people
wanted to expand a nearby pool deck before summer.
The forgetting had already started. Nobody spoke
of the spruce and those who arrived later

would not know its story. Soon there would be flagstone
over the site where its roots once stood. And every day she fasted,
fasting would be easier. Her body could forget hunger as she learned
a new landscape. She could get used to emptiness
but for that tree's insistence in air, the smell of spruce
resinous and green.

# Recolouring the Map

*a climate innovation poem, celebrating the Arcadia Education Project*
*on the banks of the Dhaleshwari River in South Kanarchor, Bangladesh*

[TORONTO/DHAKA]

A city girl, I went to school
    in a watershed far from the river
        of that age between stream and sea

when I felt the levees of my life
    most keenly. My teacher gave me
        a map, the kind with contours only

and I coloured the land green and
    water blue because I knew nothing
        of floodplains, my school solidly

on the ground, where we played
    tag and hopscotch and tetherball.
        Away, born high in the Himalayas

snow-fed with summer melt
    flowing down foothill, across
        plain, an old river with an appetite

for rain, swallows monsoons and
    bends past a school built on a base
        of upcycled tires, empty steel drums

with three types of bamboo
    rope-tied with skilled and patient
        hands — floors, roof, and walls where

light slips through the weave
    waterproofed with *gaab* fruit
        pulled from its peel and boiled down

down to where kids play on a platform
        open to sky, and when ancient water
                flows over its banks, the school floats

                floats on the river        not flooding but        *breathing*

                    ❧

# The Kite

[INDIA, C. 1947]

It had a bridle and a flying line,
string that wound
around a spool held
by many hands.

When the string
was cut

the laws of physics
meant three forces
grappled with its bamboo frame
till gravity prevailed.

A paper diamond in the sky, growing
larger and larger in the collective eye —

falling

past the glossy crows
past the jackfruit tree
past the guava tree

into a compound
where a child and his cousin played.

My father's memory
has slipped through the sieve of time.
He does not remember
the colours of the kite, only that he
and his cousin fought because of it.

The sun and the sky and the soil —
everything was the same,
but in the falling of the kite
a rivalry was made.

## The Line You Approach Infinitely

My Calculus teacher
explained asymptotes like this:
*Imagine a line, yourself,*
*one stride away from that line. Take a step.*
*Another — but each time close*
*only half the distance. You could journey*

*forever.* When summer sets in the north,
monarch butterflies skirt
the Sierra Madre, wing 2000 miles
to Mexico. It's an orange commotion
Doppler reads as weather. They arrive

on the Day of the Dead, day
of the dancing skulls. Fishermen
draw nets through night air to usher

the returning. In the oyamel forest,
monarchs weighing less than paperclips
vault into a cathedral of wings, cling
to warm wood and needle for months
before flying north,

dying — lifespan, the length
of their most necessary journey.

*One down, 47 more,* you wrote.
You finished your manuscript, and I was on a train
between two stations when your migration
ended. We had traded poems. You urged me
to cut the last line.

# The Parrot

[EAST PAKISTAN, C. 1958]

Daily

a typist woke to piecework & wage        fingers fell upon those keys

like rain, lifting

    weary hammers from their beds. Spooling &

unspooling, the ribbon knew infinity        while the carriage stopped at the end of the line.

      Keys *clack-clacking*, a page        shifting higher on the platen.

Over the typist's shoulder hung

        a cage, inside it, a parrot gifted in mimicry
        green with an orange beak *clack-clacking*.

Far from the forests, the fruit & flowers & squabbling flock

the parrot preened on a slim perch
ate red chillies, lived calmly

till the typist fell ill, sold the bird to a boy.

Dhaka to Rajshahi, in the care of his sister on a train

the parrot in the carriage kept *clack-clacking.*

But when the steam train

jerked, whistled kettle–like
the parrot beat its wings against the wires —

A story my mother told me

about a bird in a cage in a train, frightened
of the train.

15

# The Well

[RAJSHAHI, EAST PAKISTAN, C. 1958]

The cat had fallen in again,
pale brown paws slipping
from the well's circumference.

Four guava trees stood by.
Thin-limbed, a child ran
and her voice flew

from the roost of her throat.
She called for Khalil,
who was from Noakhali

but lived on the other side
of the wall, in a Hindu family's
once-home.

They shared the well in the wall:
two ropes, two pails
and a metal partition.

The cat was mewling —
Khalil fed a rope through his hands
and the child's voice

lowered like the pail
into which the cat clambered.
A slow haul. The cat

shook dry its body, and the day
was ruffled as the frock
the child smoothed down.

Khalil and the child
stood on opposite sides of a divided well
but the water drawn was the same.

16

The child would become my mother.
This was after Partition,
before the Liberation War, not far

from a stream that split from a river
and changed its name.

## Echoes, Assynt

[SCOTLAND, AUGUST 2014/1960]

On the fifth day, I climbed Cnoc Breac and stood before the moor—the *lochs* and *burns* and *smirr*—before the footpaths and a winding road—generations of rocks, young and old leaving signatures—on land whose story I was learning—sandstone on a bed of gneiss—Suilven and Canisp, island mountains shaped by ice and time—I stood before a *cèilidh* of earth and sky /

　　　　　　　　Over a half-century ago, my father flew from East Pakistan to study in Britain—bought a motorbike second-hand (Triumph Tiger Cub!)—put a learner's plate over the rear wheel—neatly roped his rucksack to the seat—Wanderlust took him to the western coast—(Did I know? My memory deep and stratified)—He had a trench coat and knew that *loch* meant *lake*—A postcard of Lochinver dated August 1960 in my father's hand—shows Suilven and Canisp from the other side—where a village hums quietly by the grass—and two mountains keep records of their past.

18

# Hurricanes

[DHAKA, EAST PAKISTAN, MARCH 1971]

That is what my mother called the lanterns,
one in every room,
kerosene already funnelled
into their metal founts.

Her father had taught her how to light one,
to wait for oil rising
through the burner's cotton wick, like courage
through a body.

To raise the globe of glass,
carry a match, its small head on fire.

He would not live to see the civil war,
the patrolling army and nightly curfews,
my mother a soft syllable stepping

out of the living room,
its four windows curtained.
On the wall, my grandmother's painting of *choka* —
shelducks with bright bodies
disappearing in the dark interior.
They lit one lantern.


Years later,
she's still grasping the bail,
holding history like a hurricane
whose wick she trims and trims.


A war of liberation —

                     two winds

                              swirling over water.

    When the storm spirals home

                                    she stays upright, lit.

# The Wind

that moves
through my grandmother's poems
is southern (দক্ষিণ) or southerly (দক্ষিণ দিকে).

I keep forgetting:
are winds named for their origin
or direction?

Far from my origin,
I sound Bangla words slowly
and they stumble
from my mouth like fawns.

Wind is air migrating.
Wind is my mother running

her finger down the page
of a Bangla-to-English dictionary.

I began by learning vowels
that transform
according to their surroundings:
from আ to া and ই to ি and ঈ to ী

My grandmother's poems name:
দোয়েল (doyel)
রজনীগন্ধা (tuberose)
হিজল (hijol)
শাপলা (waterlily)

My poems name:
peregrine
rose
pear
waterlily

Waterlilies in my poems
are only metaphorical.

My grandmother's
are laced into garlands, know
the wind.

In English, my mother asks:
*Where does the wind go?*
but I hear *belong?*

Neither there nor here
I stretch myself,
by an open mouth
am being sounded out:

a vowel
between two continents
changing shape.

# Waterlilies

*... the waterlilies fill with rain until
they overturn, spilling water into water,
then rock back, and fill with more.*

Li-Young Lee, 'I Ask My Mother to Sing'


Seeing the painting with two pink blooms
    my mother points to one, says: *shapla* —
                slips past memory's metal gate
    to her house in *Dhaka*, a *pond*
      of waterlilies visible from the *verandah*

where *early mornings* she sat
    in a *folding chair* with her *father*
           delighting in *shapla.*
    I am typically the tour guide
      talking about artists and their style.

My mind's rough canvas — stretched, primed
    filled with university lectures —
           suddenly sun-dappled
    and doubled in the deepening *pond*
      my western learnings painted over, as I sit

in the lit *verandah* of my mother's voice
    delighting in *shapla* in *Dhaka*
           my grandfather beside us
    in a *folding chair.*
    Who holds the paintbrush here?

My mother is an original
    and I, a hybrid bloom
           in this liquid mirror of red lakes
    lead white, ultramarine, viridian
      cobalt violet, brushstrokes repeating

till she rocks back, says that is all
    there is to say about the painting
           leads us to the next room.

## Projapoti

Or *butterfly* in my tongue. Grandmother,
one fluttered over a potted plant
inside your home. By the grille, the wall
that was not wall but half window, creatures
flying in and out as they please, the way
all traffic flows in Bengal. Wings
wider than my seven-year-old palms,
iridescent opal and green. Grandmother,
you bore a birthmark like a butterfly
symmetrical across your spine. As you
bent, embroidered my initials into the corner
of a kerchief, a hidden part of you
shimmered, was fluttering. I wanted
*projapoti* to land on a leaf and stay. It flew
through the grille, my very first and last
sighting.

## Notes

'An Animal in a Two-Piece Shell' is a found poem, a collage of words and phrases from *Seashells: Bivalves of the British and Northern European Seas*, by J. Møller Christensen, revised and adapted by S. Peter Dance (Penguin, 1980). A few words have been added or slightly altered to aid flow.

In 1982, the spelling of 'Dacca' changed to 'Dhaka.' In this collection, 'Dhaka' is used for all years.

# Acknowledgements

An earlier version of 'Low-Lying Country' appeared in *wildness*, Eco Folio.

'An Animal in a Two-Piece Shell' first appeared in *Invisible Zoos: Poems with a life of their own* (Eithon Bridge Publications, 2019).

'Lunar Eclipse' was shortlisted for the 2022 Oxford Brookes International Poetry Prize. The poem first appeared in *Bad Lilies* Issue Thirteen.

An earlier version of 'The Line You Approach Infinitely' appeared in *wildness*, Issue No. 6.

An earlier version of 'Echoes, Assynt' appeared at The Red Head Gallery, in the exhibition *Post Me a Card*.

'Projapoti' first appeared in *Canthius*, Issue 4.

Thank you to the editors, designers, judges, and exhibition makers for their dedication.

To Joseph O. Legaspi and my *Orion* poetry workshop peers, for their generous reading and feedback on 'Salt' and on the poem that became 'On the First Day of Ramadan.'

To Hoa Nguyen, for the workshop that released 'Low-Lying Country.'

To David Morley and Pascale Petit, for a wonderful week at Tŷ Newydd and sparking 'An Animal in a Two-Piece Shell.' To Sharon Larkin and Simon Williams, for making an anthology and giving the poem a home.

To Karen Solie and my poetry workshop peers, for their generous reading and feedback on 'Girl Made of Shells.'

To Kelley and Lauren, for reading those early lines of 'Lunar Eclipse' and pushing me forwards with enthusiasm and questions.

To Rayyan, for double-checking my Bangla.

To Lynn Crosbie, for the workshop that released 'Projapoti.'

To **ignition**press, for supporting and celebrating emerging poets: Les Robinson, Claire Cox, and Tolu Agbelusi for their eagle eyes and fresh perspectives. Niall Munro, for giving these poems generous attention and care through two seasons, and for helping me bring what was most important to the fore.

To my friends, thank you for your companionship through life and creativity.

Above all, love and gratitude to my family, for inspiration and permission to put private moments into the public sphere: My brother-in-law, for laughter. My sister, for showing me that a life with poetry is possible. My mother, who is and has always been a poem. And my grandparents and father, who keep passing poems down—I'm listening.

MIX
Paper from
responsible sources
FSC® C007326